G[illegible] Hopper

Computer Pioneer

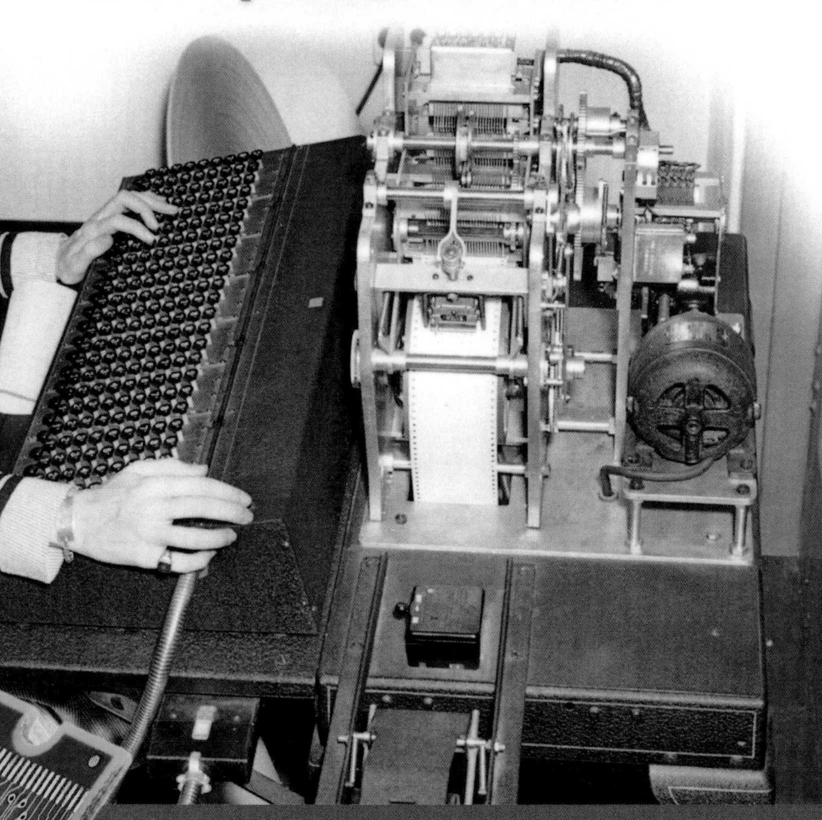

By Peggy Thomas

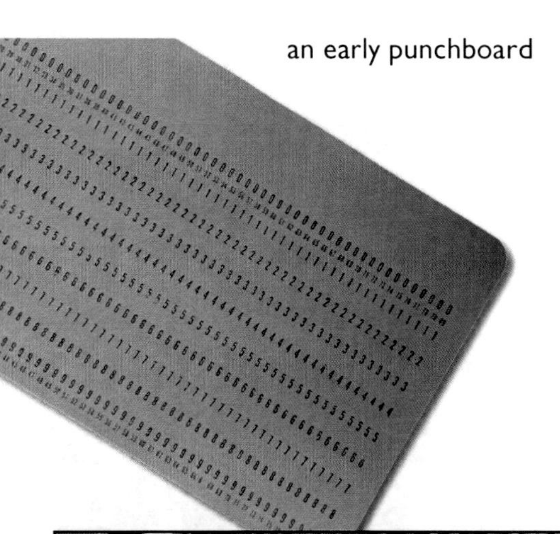

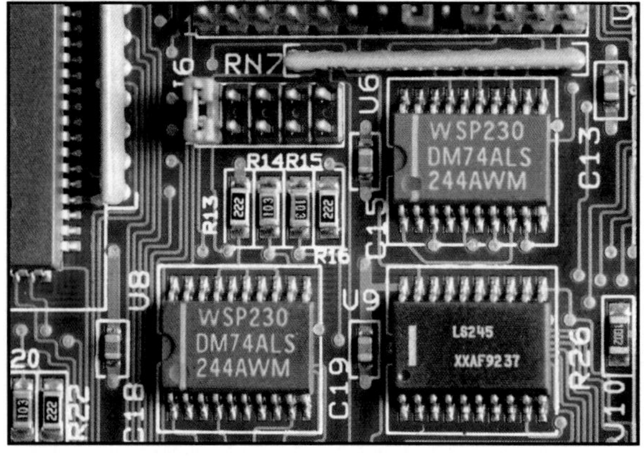

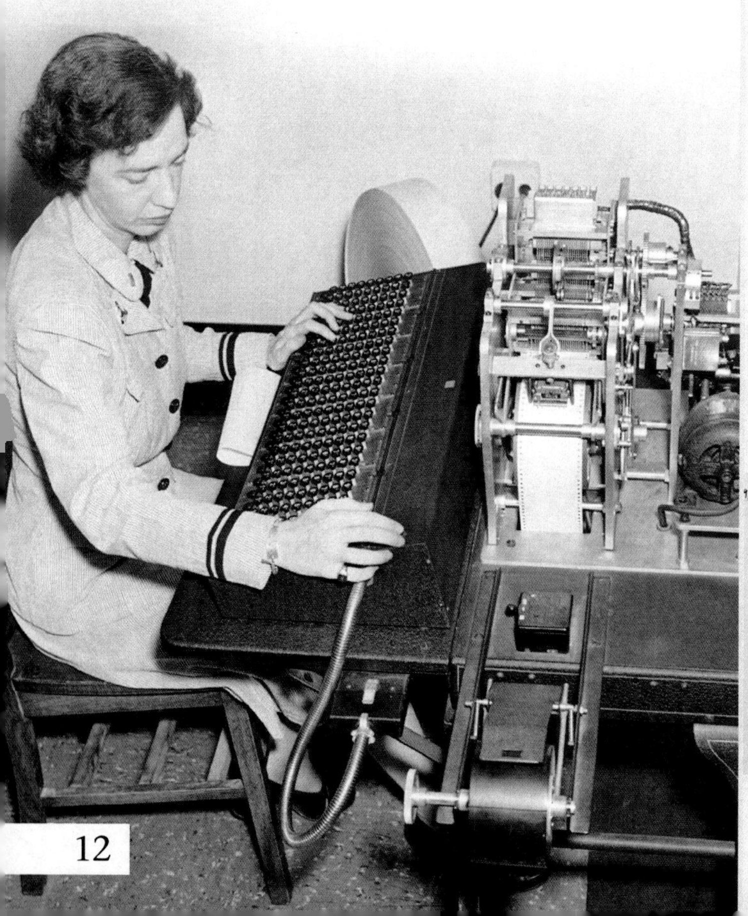

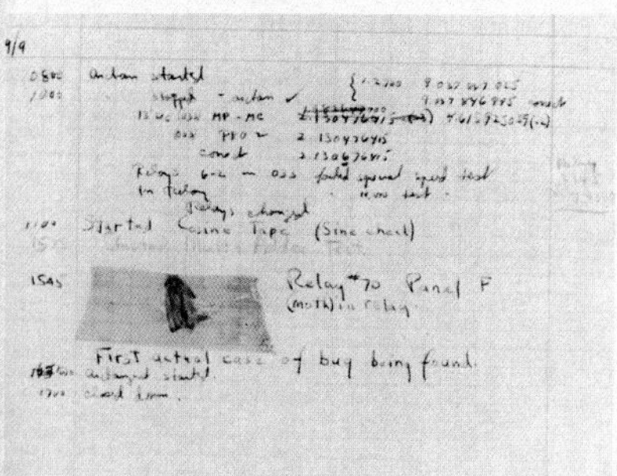

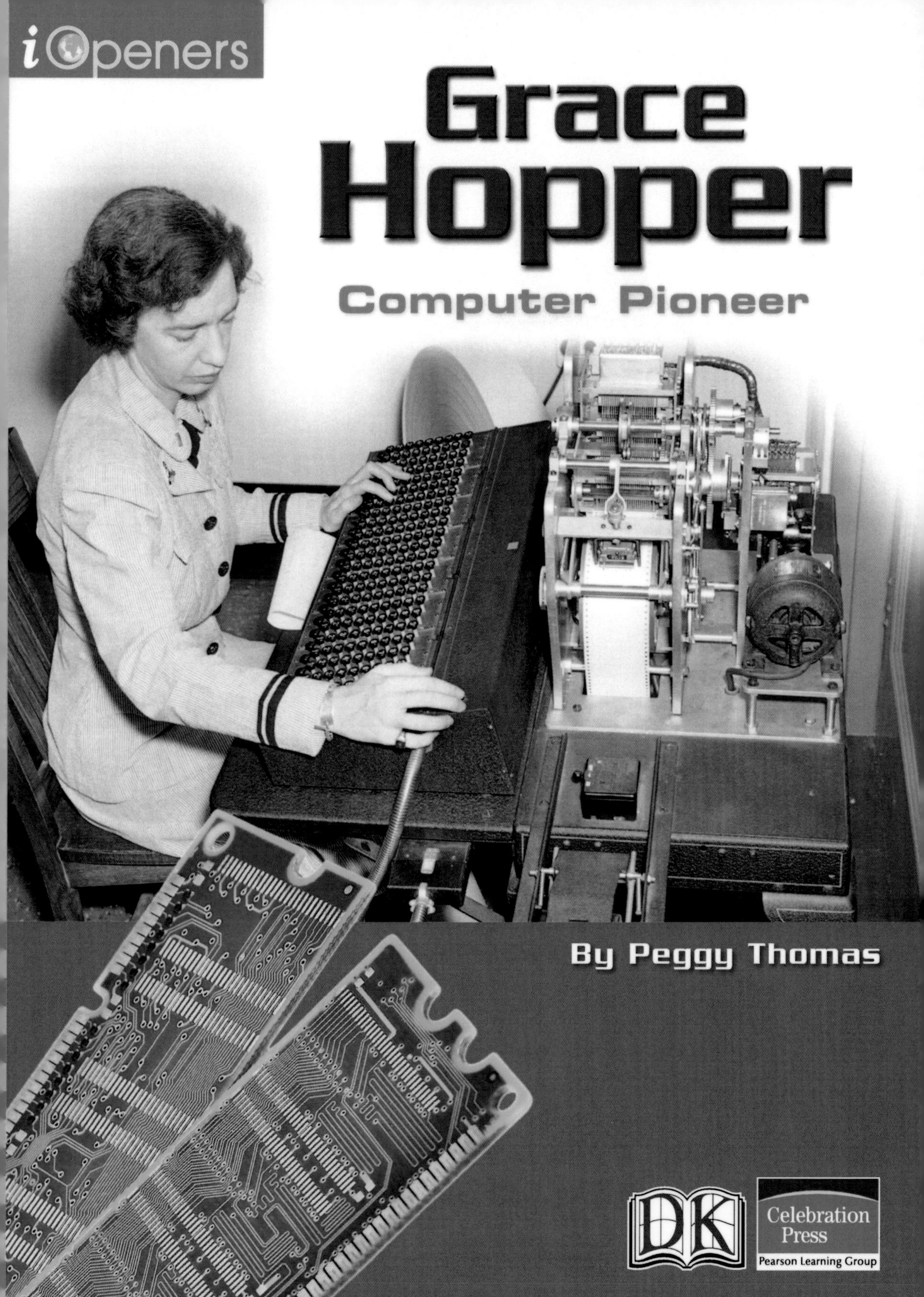
iOpeners
Grace Hopper
Computer Pioneer
By Peggy Thomas
DK
Celebration Press
Pearson Learning Group

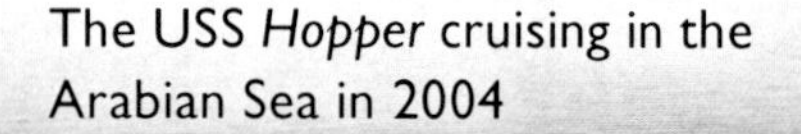

Think About It

1. Why do you think the author began the book with a story about Grace's childhood?
2. What skills do you think Grace needed to learn to compile lines of code in programming languages?
3. Why do you think the author included a diagram to show the displacement of water?
4. In what ways was Grace Hopper a pioneer?
5. What did you learn from reading this book?

DRA Level	50
Guided Reading Level	T
Lexile® Measure	850L

Nonfiction Genre
Biography/Autobiography

NCTM Standard
Data Analysis and Probability

Comprehension Skill
Identify Cause and Effect

Nonfiction Features
Boldface, Captions, Contents, Diagrams, Glossary, Headings, Index, Sidebars, Timeline

Grace Hopper: Computer Pioneer is a biography of a mathematician who worked on the first computer. This book tells about Grace Murray Hopper's extraordinary life and her contributions to the field of computer science.

1-800-321-3106
www.pearsonlearning.com

ISBN-13: 978-0-7652-8628-4
ISBN-10: 0-7652-8628-9

iOpeners

Grace Hopper

Computer Pioneer

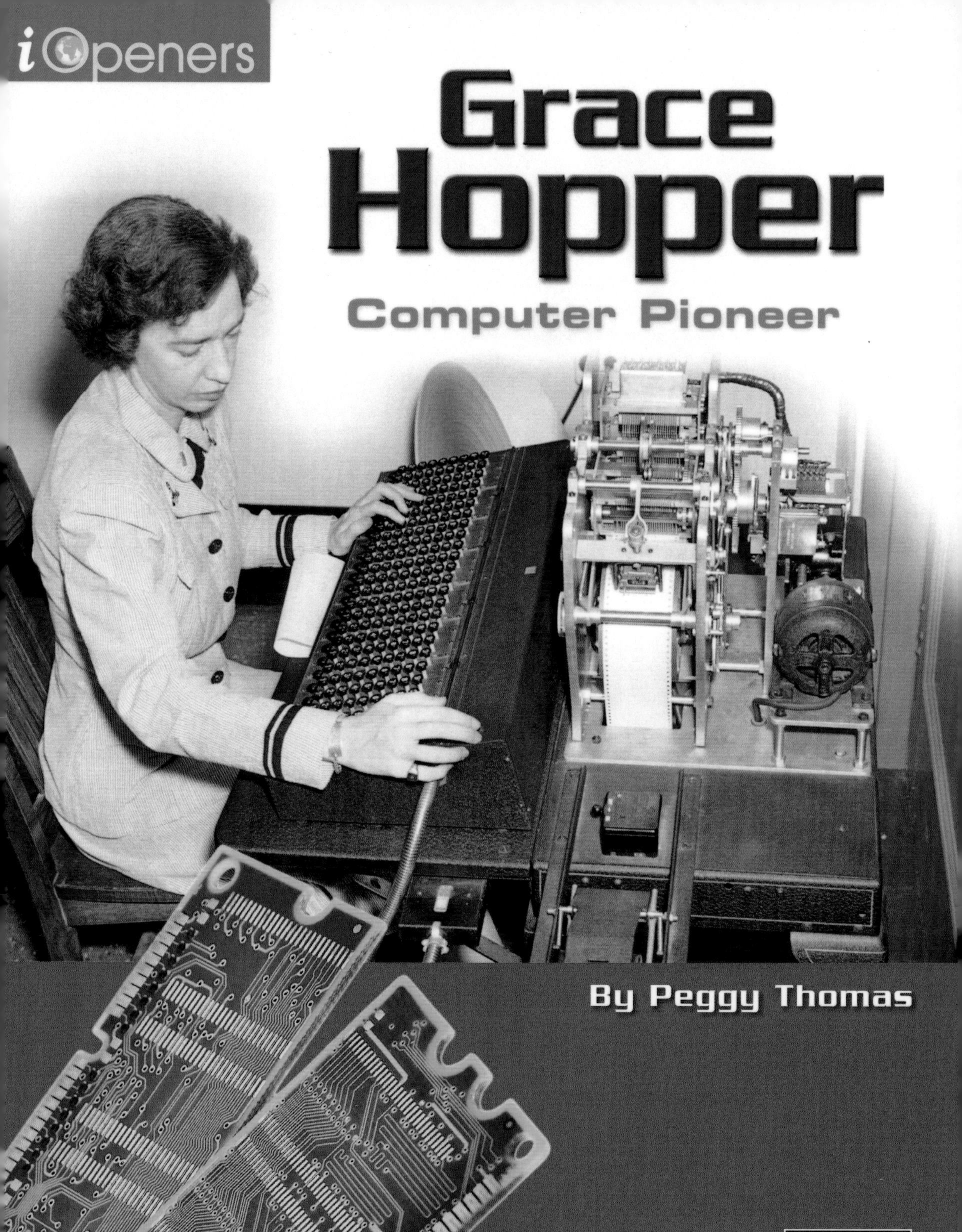

By Peggy Thomas

The following people from **Pearson Learning Group** have contributed to the development of this product:

Design Tricia Battipede, Evelyn Bauer, Robert Dobaczewski, Jennifer Visco
Marketing Kimberly Doster, Gina Konopinski-Jacobia
Editorial Leslie Feierstone Barna, Madeline Boskey Olsen, Jennifer Van Der Heide
Production Irene Belinsky, Mark Cirillo, Roxanne Knoll, Ruth Leine, Susan Levine
Visual Acquisitions Mindy Klarman, David Mager, Judy Mahoney, Salita Mehta, Elbaliz Mendez, Alison O'Brien, Dan Thomas
Content Area Consultant Mary Ann Zagar

The following people from **DK** have contributed to the development of this product:

Managing Art Director Richard Czapnik
Project Manager Nigel Duffield
Editorial Lead Heather Jones
Design Ann Cannings

All photography © Pearson Education, Inc. (PEI) unless otherwise specifically noted.

Photographs: Every effort has been made to secure permission and provide appropriate credit for photographic material. The publisher deeply regrets any omission and pledges to correct errors called to its attention in subsequent editions.

Photo locators denoted as follows: Top (T), Center (C), Bottom (B), Left (L), Right (R), Background (Bkgd)

Picture Credits: CVR(T) Bettmann/Corbis, **CVR(B)** Hellen Sergeyeva/Fotolia; **BCVR** Library of Congress; **1** AP Images; **1(T)–24(T)** Stockbyte; **2** Maglara/Fotolia; **3(L)** Library of Congress, **3(R)** Paul Bricknell/©DK Images; **4(L)** Poles/Fotolia, **4(R)** Kelly, Piet & Co./Library of Congress; **5** Dave Rudkin/DK Images; **6** Detroit Publishing Co./Library of Congress; **9(B)** Library of Congress, **9(T)** INTERFOTO/Alamy; **10(L)** Library of Congress, **10(R)** Siegel, Arthur S.,/Library of Congress; **11** ©DK Images; **12(L)** Bettmann/Corbis, **12(R)** Naval Surface Warfare Center/US Naval Historical Center; **13** Lawrence Manning/Corbis; **14(T)** Danny Daniels/Index Stock Imagery, Inc., **14(BL)** Ferenc Szelepcsenyi/Fotolia, **14(BR)** Erica Guilane-Nachez/Fotolia; **15(T)** Library of Congress, **15(B)** ASSOCIATED PRESS/AP Images; **18** Hiller, Herman/Library of Congress; **19(B)** David C. MacLean/National History & Heritage Command/Naval Historical Center, **19(T)** Frontpage/Shutterstock; **20** Andrzej Tokarski/Fotolia; **21** Cynthia Johnson/Time & Life Pictures/Getty Images; **22(B)** Aaron Peterson, USN/The Defense Visual Information Center, **22(T)** U.S. Navy Visual News Service.

Illustrations: 7, 13, 17, 20: Argosy Publishing.

ISBN-13: 978-0-7652-8628-4
ISBN-10: 0-7652-8628-9

Printed in the United States of America
5 6 7 8 9 10 V0SV 16 15 14

1-800-321-3106
www.pearsonlearning.com

Grace Hopper

By
Peggy Thomas

CELEBRATION PRESS
Pearson Learning Group

Contents

A Curious Girl

Machines fascinated young Grace Murray. When she was only seven years old, she unscrewed the back of a windup clock to find out how it worked. The gears sprang out of the casing. Grace was not discouraged. She simply collected the other six windup alarm clocks in the house and opened them, too. Each time the pieces fell out before she could see how they fit together to put them back in place. When her mother found out, she took away all but one clock for Grace to experiment on.

Years later, Grace would remember this event when she began working with a much more complex machine. It was the first **computer** in the United States.

Grace Murray's hometown was New York City.

Grace took apart seven clocks to find out how they worked.

No Limits

Grace's behavior was unusual for girls who were born in 1906. At that time, girls were expected to learn how to run a household and be good wives. However, her parents believed that Grace and her brother and sister should learn about everything. Perhaps they knew how difficult life could be when a person was limited in what he or she could do. They bought Grace a metal construction kit, and she tinkered with machines while other girls played with dolls.

Grace built models of working elevators and moving cars with her construction kit.

"Remember Your Great-Grandfather!"

Grace was always encouraged to do her best. When she was learning to sail by herself, her mother watched from shore. Once, a strong wind tipped the boat over. Her mother yelled out, "Remember your great-grandfather, the admiral!" Grace did. She clung to the boat and pushed it back to shore. Perhaps she imagined what her great-grandfather would have done. He was a Navy rear admiral in the Civil War.

a Civil War Naval battle

When Grace was young, her father, Walter Murray, had to have his legs removed from the knees down because of artery disease. It was a long and difficult recovery. Walter Murray did not let anything get in his way. He went back to work at his insurance company. He puttered in his workshop and even played golf.

Grace's mother, Mary Murray, took over many of her husband's duties. At that time, few families owned a car and fewer women knew how to drive. Mrs. Murray bought a car, learned how to drive, and drove her husband to work every day. She also loved math. So, she took over paying the bills. She figured out the taxes and kept track of accounts while Grace looked on.

Grace's mother drove a Model T like the one shown here.

Grace, the Student

Standing as still as she could, Grace held the tall red-and-white striped pole for her grandfather, John Van Horne. He was a **surveyor** who measured the surface of the land and planned new streets in New York City.

Holding the pole was an important job. If Grace let the pole tilt, her grandfather might **calculate** angles incorrectly. Then, the streets would not be straight. While helping her grandfather, Grace learned to measure curves, angles, and straight lines. She enjoyed seeing them turn into streets, sidewalks, and parks.

In school, Grace excelled in math. In 1923, at the age of seventeen, she applied to Vassar College. When she failed the Latin portion of the entrance exam, Grace went to another school and worked hard on Latin. The following spring, Grace took the exam again and passed.

Grace studied math and physics at Vassar College in Poughkeepsie, New York.

Bathtub Science

In the 1920s, many young women took classes in art, history, and English. However, Grace majored in mathematics and physics, the study of energy and matter.

Sometimes, her friends needed help understanding difficult lessons in math. Grace invented interesting ways to teach them. She once demonstrated the theory of **displacement** by lowering a student into a bathtub. By doing so, she showed how water in a container moves up and around an object that is dropped into it. The level depends on the object's volume.

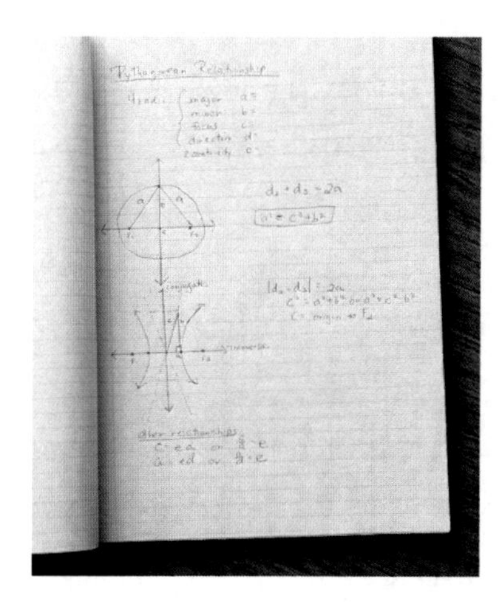

Grace studied math and physics.

Displacement of Water

The level of water in a container will rise according to the volume of the objects dropped into it. Try it yourself. Fill a glass partway with water. Drop several coins into the water. Did the water level rise? Add more coins and see what happens.

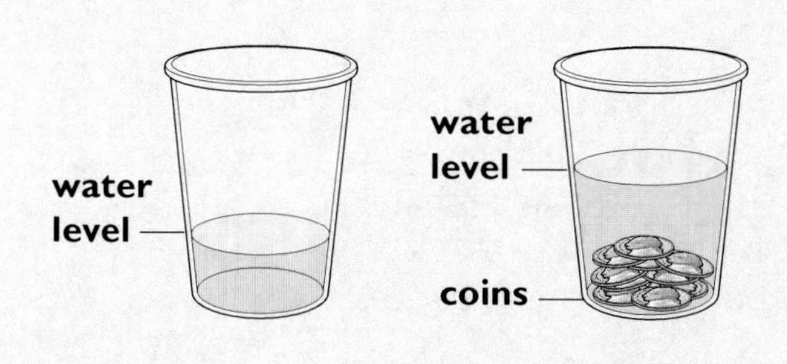

A Terrific Teacher

During one summer break, Grace met Vincent Hopper. They married in 1930, shortly after Grace earned her master's degree in mathematics from Yale University. At the time, married women were not expected to work. However, Grace began teaching in the Vassar math department. She taught trigonometry, which is the study of triangles and their properties, and calculus, which uses symbols in mathematical **equations**.

Grace tried to show her students the importance of math in everyday life. To learn **probability**, they played card games and other games. In other classes, they planned buildings. They mapped cities and calculated the cost to run them.

Grace used objects like these number cubes to teach probability.

When Grace was not teaching a class at Vassar, she continued studying math at Yale. In 1934, she earned her **doctorate** degree in math.

Probability

Probability is the chance that a specific event will occur compared to the number of possible outcomes. Roll a number cube once. What is the chance that it will land on the number 4? There are six sides to a number cube and only one number 4. Your chances are 1 out of 6.

A Navy WAVE

On December 7, 1941, Grace was listening to the radio. She heard the news that Japanese forces had bombed Pearl Harbor in Hawaii. The United States soon entered World War II. Every citizen was called into action.

Millions of American men left their jobs and went off to war. Some women stepped into factory jobs, building planes and tanks. Others **enlisted** in the newly formed Navy WAVES, which stood for Women Accepted for Volunteer Emergency Service. These enlisted women worked in Navy offices so that men could go into battle.

Honolulu Star-Bulletin 1st EXTRA

WAR!

(Associated Press by Transpacific Telephone)

SAN FRANCISCO, Dec. 7.—President Roosevelt announced this morning that Japanese planes had attacked Manila and Pearl Harbor.

OAHU BOMBED BY JAPANESE PLANES

SIX KNOWN DEAD, 21 INJURED, AT EMERGENCY HOSPITAL

Attack Made On Island's Defense Areas

Hundreds See City Bombed

Names of Dead and Injured

Schools Closed

Editorial

The United States entered the war after the attack on Pearl Harbor on December 7, 1941.

Lieutenant Hopper

Grace wanted to enlist. The Navy said that by their rules Grace was underweight and too old. She was thirty-five. They also said her work as a teacher of mathematics was too important for her to do an office job in the military. She was needed to teach math to others who would be joining the military. They needed mathematics to understand the new technology used in the war.

Grace requested a leave of absence from Vassar. Then, she convinced the recruitment officers that she was fit for duty. In December 1943, she was sworn in to the WAVES and sent for training. Upon graduation, Lieutenant Grace Hopper was given her first official assignment. She was sent to Harvard University in Cambridge, Massachusetts, to work with a brand-new machine called a computer.

Women were accepted into the Navy to serve during World War II. Grace joined the WAVES in 1943.

Amazing Grace Meets Mark I

In 1944, most people had never heard of a computer. Grace had only read about them. When she got to the lab, she remembered, "There was this large mass of machinery out there making a lot of racket.... All I could do was look at it, I couldn't think of anything to say." The computer was called Mark I. It was a giant that stood 8 feet high, weighed about 5 tons, and covered all the walls of a large room.

On one end, four reels of paper tape fed the machine its program, or instructions. Typewriters at the other end recorded the information the computer put out. In between, 500 miles of wire connected nearly 800,000 parts that clicked and whizzed.

The First Computers

The first computers were based on the work of other inventors like Charles Babbage. In the 1800s, he designed a calculator called the Difference Engine. It was powered by steam and calculated problems by turning cogs and gears.

the Difference Engine

The Navy hoped that Mark I would provide fast information that would help them win the war. The enemy in Germany had a similar machine, so speed was essential. Mark I calculated the strength of metals to see which ones should be used in ship construction. It computed the distance and angles of rocket launches. It also figured the effectiveness of magnetic mines.

These calculations were usually done by hand. Human calculators could not keep up with the demand. Mark I worked faster. It ran 24 hours a day every day without getting tired.

Grace working on the Mark I

Debugging the System

Early computers frequently jammed for many reasons. When a moth jammed the system, Grace and another programmer fished it out and taped it into the lab's logbook. After that, it was common to call fixing a computer problem "debugging."

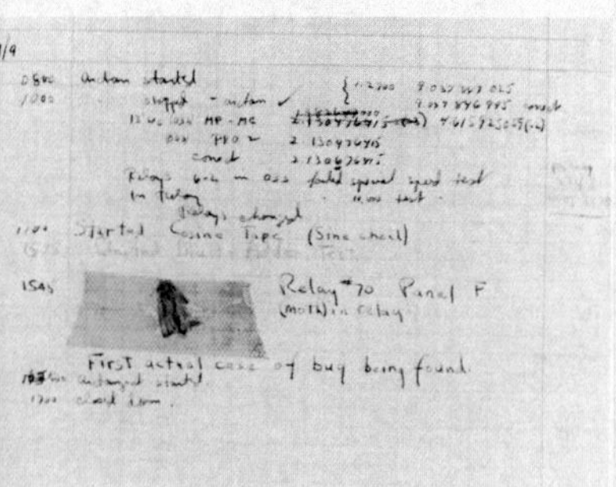
9/9

1545 Relay #70 Panel F
(moth) in relay.

First actual case of bug being found.

the "computer bug"

The Programming Process

For every problem, Grace first had to figure out the mathematical equation that would provide the answers they needed. Then, she had to break down the equation into small step-by-step instructions of addition, subtraction, multiplication, or division. In the third step, Grace translated the equation into language that the computer could understand.

Mark I worked on two signals: "switch ON" and "switch OFF." To signal the switches, it used only two numbers: 0 and 1. This two-digit system was called the **binary code**.

The Binary Code

0	0000
1	0001
2	0010
3	0011
4	0100
5	0101
6	0110
7	0111
8	1000
9	1001

In this two-digit system, numbers and letters are represented by 0s and 1s.

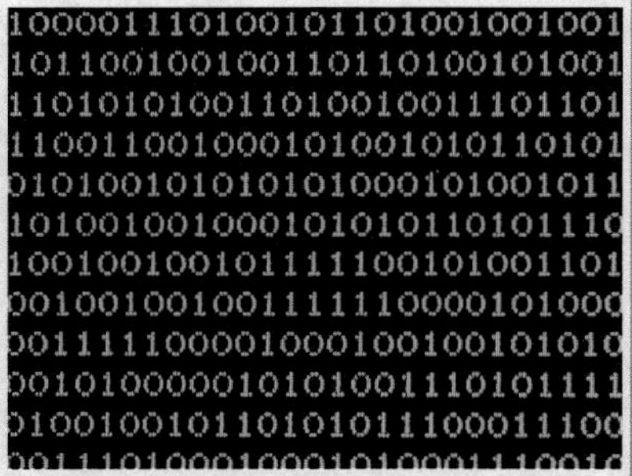

binary code in action

Simple Binary Circuit

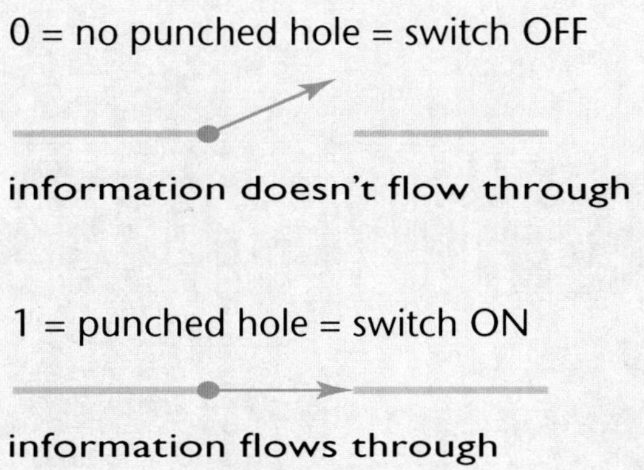

0 = no punched hole = switch OFF

information doesn't flow through

1 = punched hole = switch ON

information flows through

Once Grace had the instructions written in binary code, she then had to translate the code so Mark I could read it. This was done using a series of punched holes in reels of paper tape that were fed into the computer. A punched hole indicated a 1. A space with no hole indicated a 0. Mark I read the punched holes as "switch ON." It read 0s or no holes as "switch OFF." This process took a lot of time. Even so, programming Mark I was faster and more accurate than figuring out the computations by hand.

By 1945, Grace was working on a faster machine. Mark II performed tasks five times faster than Mark I.

Holes of Information

The early computers were programmed using holes punched in rolls of paper tape or cards. This idea was borrowed from Joseph-Marie Jacquard. In 1802, he programmed weaving looms with thousands of cards punched with the pattern to be woven.

an early punchboard

a simple binary circuit

the Jacquard loom

Grandmother of COBOL

World War II ended in 1945.

In 1945, the United States and its allies won the war. Grace stayed on in the Navy, working part-time as a computer consultant and speaker. She also worked at Harvard, programming a new computer called Mark III.

Her duties included creating mathematical tables and charts to help other scientists. She would rather have taught the scientists how to use the computers. However, people believed that only mathematicians could understand the codes to operate the complex machines.

In Grace's mind, a code was just a series of symbols. It didn't matter if those symbols were numbers, multiplication signs, or letters of the alphabet. Grace insisted that programs could be written for the ordinary person to use. So, she left Harvard and joined a company that built and sold computers to businesses.

the Mark III at Harvard in 1949

The First Compiler

In 1949, Grace became the senior programmer at Eckert-Mauchly Computer Corporation. There, she helped create the smallest computer ever built up until that time—UNIVAC. It was 14½ feet long, 8½ feet high, and 7½ feet wide. Although it was much smaller than Mark III, UNIVAC performed much faster. It also had an internal memory so that it could remember simple programs that were stored inside.

Grace believed that a computer with that kind of power should be able to gather or compile its own programming instructions. Even the most difficult math problems could be broken down into simple instruction sets or **subroutines**. These subroutines could be used over and over. Instead of writing the codes many times, Grace gave each subroutine a three-letter name. The computer could call the name from its instruction tapes.

Basic Subroutines

addition	A + B = C	ADD subroutine
subtraction	A – B = C	SUB subroutine
multiplication	A x B = C	MUL subroutine
division	A / B = C	DIV subroutine

Timeline of Grace Hopper's Life

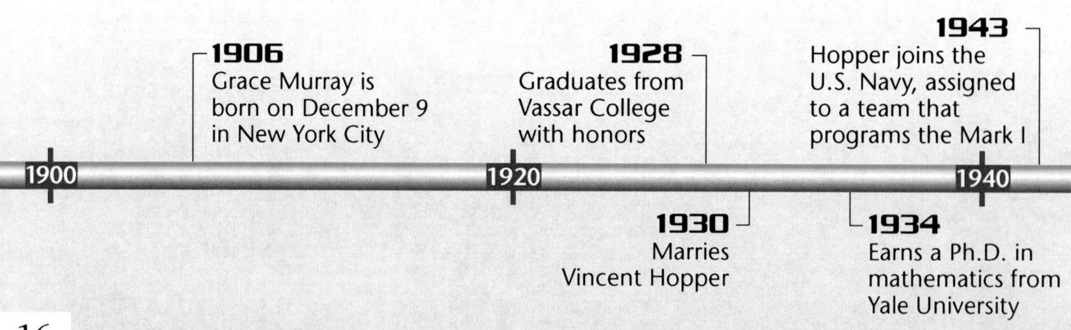

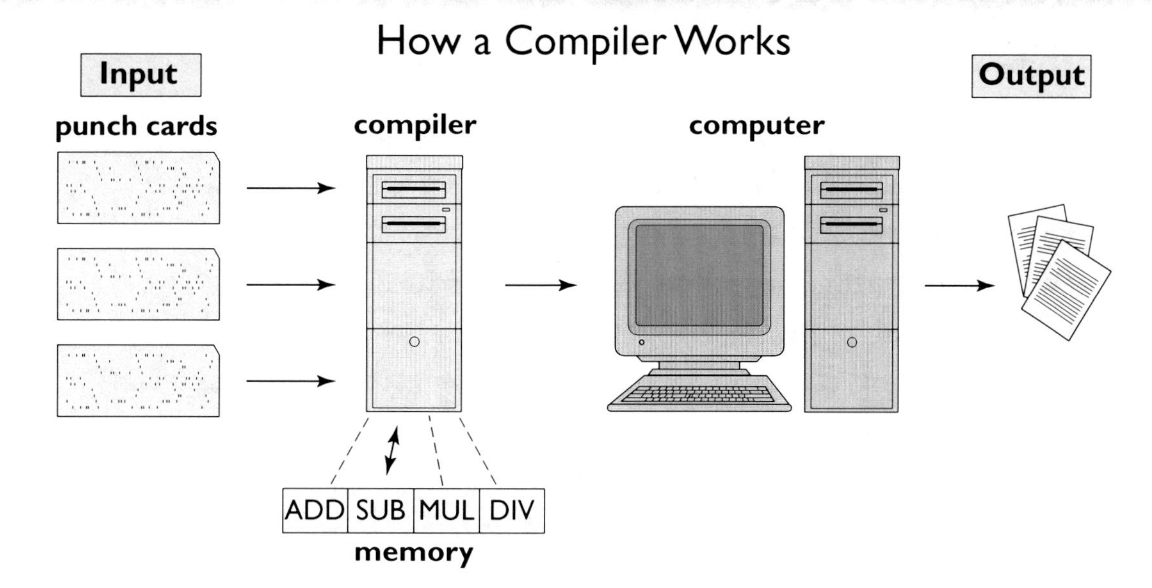

For example, a SUB subroutine told the computer to subtract one number from another. It then stored the answer in a special location. Later, the computer could be told to "pick up" the answer and use it in further computations.

Grace called this process a **compiler**. Like a person in a library collecting books to read, the computer gathered or compiled all the subroutines it needed to run the program. This was a big achievement. It meant that programs that once took a month to write now took the computer about five minutes to compile. Grace could turn her attention to making computers more "user friendly" by using the English language.

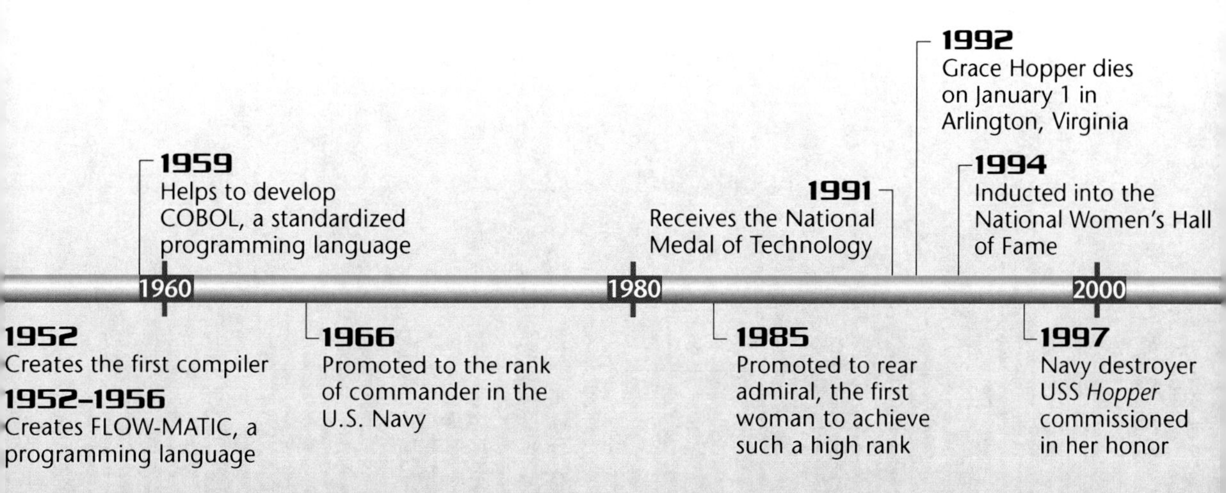

Computers for Ordinary People

By 1956, Grace had designed the first programs that used words like *input, file, compare, read, write, data,* and *stop.* She called her computer languages simply A-0 and B-0. The UNIVAC salesman called them MATH-MATIC and FLOW-MATIC. They were a hit. For the first time, ordinary people were using computers. Insurance companies, stores, and even the U.S. Census Bureau, which was in charge of counting the population, used UNIVAC.

Three years later, FLOW-MATIC became the basis for COBOL. COBOL is short for COmmon Business Oriented Language. It is still used by businesses today. Although Grace did not invent COBOL, she advised the team that did the work. They nicknamed her the Grandmother of COBOL.

The U.S. Census Bureau was one of the first organizations to use UNIVAC.

Grace was the director of the Navy programming languages group at the Pentagon.

Grace to the Rescue

In 1966, Grace was promoted to Navy commander. However, that same year, Navy officials told her it was time to retire.

Her retirement did not last long. Seven months later, the Navy had problems with their COBOL program. They needed Grace to fix it. At age sixty-one, Grace became the director of the Navy programming languages group. She moved into a new office at the Pentagon in Washington, D.C.

Grace Hopper working at her desk

The problem was caused by individual programmers writing their own codes to solve specific problems. Each programmer's codes were different and caused a language barrier. Grace created a language that combined all the individual codes into one. It was called the USA Standard COBOL.

Doing Things Differently

Grace decorated her office with a pirate's flag.

Grace was an unusual sight at the Pentagon. She decorated her office with a pirate's skull and crossbones flag, and she encouraged people to tell time by her backward clock. The number 11 was where the 1 should be, and the number 10 was in the place of the 2. The hands also ran counterclockwise, or the opposite direction of most clocks. The clock told correct time. Grace said that it just took people a few days to realize that there was no good reason for a clock to run clockwise. Her clock and her unusual ways reminded people that there was more than one way to get a job done. This was not just something Grace told others. She lived it.

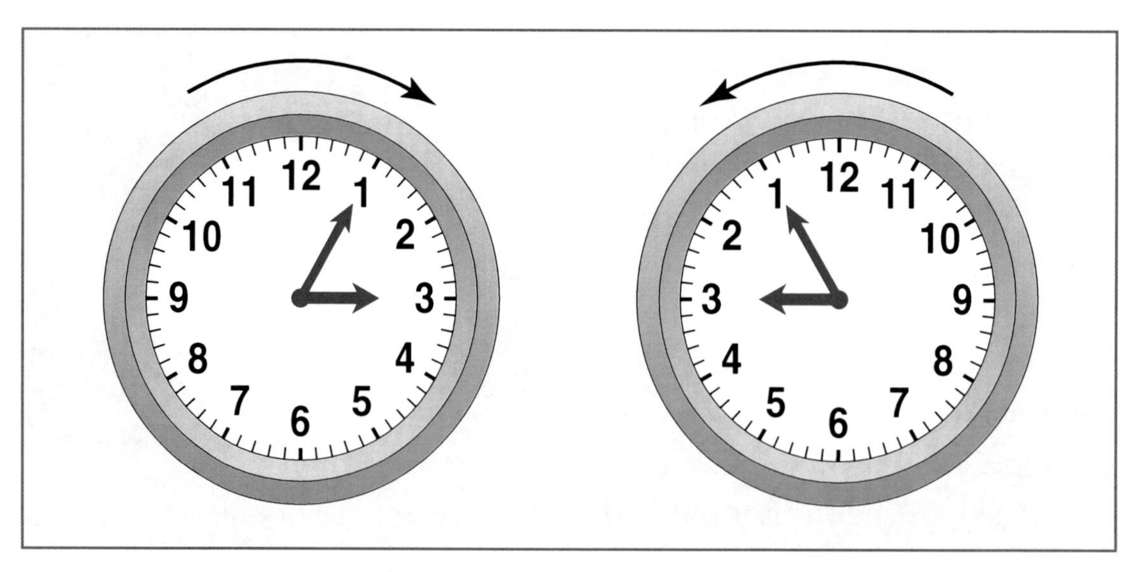

Both clocks tell perfect time. It is 3:05.

Seeing a Nanosecond

One day, Grace read about electric circuits that acted in a **nanosecond** (a billionth of a second). She could not imagine something so fast. She needed to see it to understand. Grace called an engineer and asked him to cut a length of wire that would show her how far electricity could travel in a nanosecond. The engineer sent her a length of wire 11.8 inches long. Now, she could actually see how fast electricity moved from a light switch to a lightbulb.

At the age of seventy-eight, Grace was promoted to rear **admiral**, the same rank her great-grandfather had held. A year later, in 1986, she retired from the Navy. This time it was for good. She did not stop working, though. Grace continued to speak to schools and businesses, encouraging people to use computers.

Dare and Do

Grace often told students, "A ship in port is safe, but that is not what ships are built for...Dare and do."

Her Work Lives On

On January 1, 1992, at the age of eighty-five, Admiral Grace Hopper died in her sleep. She was buried at Arlington National Cemetery in Virginia with full Navy honors. She continued to be honored even after death. In 1994, she was inducted into the National Women's Hall of Fame. In 1997, the Navy commissioned a guided missile destroyer named after her: the USS *Hopper.* More importantly, people everywhere use computers, just as Grace had once hoped they would, and so her work lives on.

Grace spoke at the groundbreaking for the Grace M. Hopper Regional Data Automation Center in North Island, California, in 1985.

The USS *Hopper* cruising in the Arabian Sea in 2004

Glossary

admiral	a high-ranking naval officer
binary code	a counting system that uses only two digits: 0 and 1
calculate	to find an answer using mathematics
compiler	the part of a computer program that collects smaller units of programming
computer	a machine designed to perform high-speed calculations and other operations
displacement	the fact that water in a container rises according to the volume of an object dropped into it
doctorate	the highest degree given in college
enlisted	signed up for military duty
equations	mathematical statements that are equal on both sides
nanosecond	a billionth of a second
probability	the chance of one event occurring over all possible outcomes
subroutines	sets of instructions that can be coded once and used many times
surveyor	a person who measures the surface of the land

Index